PSYCHIC AWAKENING SERIES
BOOK 2

TELEKINESIS

Embrosewyn Tazkuvel

OTHER CAPTIVATING, THOUGHT-PROVOKING BOOKS
by Embrosewyn Tazkuvel

WORDS OF POWER AND TRANSFORMATION
101+ Magickal Words and Sigils of Celestine Light to Manifest Your Desires

AURAS
How To See, Feel And Know

SOUL MATE AURAS
How to Use Your Aura to Find Your Soul Mate

Secret Earth Series
INCEPTION *(Book 1)*
DESTINY *(Book 2)*

Psychic Awakening Series
CLAIRVOYANCE *(Book 1)*
DREAMS *(Book 3)*

UNLEASH YOUR PSYCHIC POWERS

PSYCHIC SELF DEFENSE

LOVE YOURSELF
Secret Key To Transforming Your Life

22 STEPS TO THE LIGHT OF YOUR SOUL

ORACLES OF CELESTINE LIGHT
Complete Trilogy of Genesis, Nexus & Vivus

Published by Kaleidoscope Productions
1467 Siskiyou Boulevard, #9; Ashland, OR 97520
www.kaleidoscope-publications.com

Cover design & book layout by Sumara Elan Love
www.3wizardz.com

TABLE OF CONTENTS

AWESOME RANGE OF POWER

The ability to move or otherwise affect objects with force waves of the mind and/or aura is referred to as Telekinesis; but this is more of a modern limited perception of the word. You can do much more than move objects using the power of telekinesis. Because of its versatility, it is one of my favorite paranormal abilities and one I practice regularly to improve.

To grasp the wide range of actions that can be initiated by telekinesis, just think of what you can do with your hand. Anything you can do with your hand you can do without physically touching an object by using telekinesis. If you want to think bigger, imagine anything that a group of people could unite and physically move or affect. You can do the same thing with telekinesis. To envision on an adept level, think of anything a piece of power equipment such as a bulldozer could do. The same thing could be accomplished by an adept of telekinesis.

To fully grasp the vast extent of telekinetic capabilities, consider the following list. Some of the more advanced feats will seem like fantasy or science fiction, but there are recorded instances in history of people demonstrating all of the abilities below.

Basic Abilities

-Move a very light object such as a feather, a psi wheel, or the pages of a book.

-Slightly soften thin pieces of metal. Spoon bending with light physical manipulation on the thinner parts of the utensils would be an example.

Intermediate Abilities

-Move a heavier, but still light object such as a pencil, small book or small cup.

-Move very light objects such as a feather, a psi wheel, enclosed within a glass dome.

-Soften thin pieces of metal. With intermediate telekinetic ability the thicker parts of utensils such as the fork tines could be bent by light physical manipulation.

-Levitate a very light object such as a feather, a psi wheel, or the pages of a book.

Advanced Abilities

-Move an object that a 12 year old child could lift and carry such as a dining room chair.

-Soften thicker pieces of metal. The bowl of a thick spoon could be bent with light physical manipulation.

-Levitate a heavier, but still light object such as a

pencil or a small book in the open air.

-Levitate a light object such as a feather covered by a glass dome.

-Bind or hold in place a light object such as a feather, a psi wheel, or the pages of a book, that should move when blown upon by another person, but will not.

-Cause a sensation of physical touch on another person's body without physical contact. For instance, they may feel like they were just touched by a hand on their arm, while you are still across the room.

-Manipulate the inner workings of simple devices requiring little force. For instance, you could move the hands of a clock.

Master Abilities

-Move an object that an adult man would strain to carry.

-Greatly soften thicker pieces of metal. The bowl of a thick spoon could be bent without any physical manipulation.

-Levitate an object that a 12 year old child could lift and carry such as a dining room chair.

-Bind or hold in place a light object such as a pencil or a small book, that should move when touched by another person, but will not.

-Organize and move water in a levitated stream of

1 inch or less in diameter.

-Move yourself a short distance with your feet barely levitated above the ground without using a physical motivating force such as walking. Or levitate yourself straight up off the ground a short distance and hold yourself in position for at least 5 seconds.

-Cause physical pain to another person's body without physical contact. For instance, they may feel like they were just hit by a fist on their arm, while you are still across the room.

-Change the direction of a small moving object; for instance, alter the roll of dice after they have been thrown to turn up the numbers you desire.

-Manipulate the inner workings of more complex devices requiring little force. For instance, you could depress the keys of a calculator without physically touching it.

-Compress a weak object such as crushing a soda can without physically touching it.

-Cause objects held together with glue, nails, screws or other permanent fasteners to fall apart.

-Cause a flammable object to spontaneously catch on fire.

Adept Abilities
-Move an object that no human could normally lift or move such as a car.

-Soften a 1/4" steel plate to the point that it bends under its own weight.

-Levitate an object too heavy for a single person to physically move

-Bind or hold in place most things small to big, light to heavy, including people, against almost any non-psychic, opposing external physical force.

-Organize and move water in a levitated stream 1- 6 inches in diameter.

-Move yourself a short distance with your feet barely levitated above the ground without using a physical motivating force such as walking. Or levitate yourself straight up off the ground a short distance and hold yourself in position for at least 10 seconds.

-Cause serious physical damage to another person's body without physical contact. For instance, someone attacking you may feel like their throat is in the grasp of two hands choking them, while you may be physically immobilized. It is not an illusionary feeling but a real physical event that is occurring.

-Change the direction of a large moving object. For instance if you were in a car about to crash, you could turn the car while it was moving to avoid the collision even if you were not the driver.

-Manipulate the inner workings of fairly complex

devices. For instance, you could open a locked door without a key by manipulating the locking pins.

-Compress or bend a larger, stronger object such as crushing a computer, or bending a gun barrel without physically touching them.

-Cause objects held together by natural means such as a table top made from wooden boards, to erupt apart explosively.

-Discombobulate a person's brain by affecting the neural connection between cells.

-Cause a non-flammable object to spontaneously combust in flame.

As extensive as this list is, it is still only a partial list of telekinetic abilities. But it should be sufficient for most people to key in on the areas they want to focus on and practice.

ORIGIN OF THE WORD

The term telekinesis was first used in the late 1800's and originally did not apply to a paranormal power of humans. Instead it referred to objects moved by unseen ghosts, demons, spirits and various other supernatural forces, most often at the behest of a human spiritualist or medium.

By the early 1900's fake and fraudulent mediums were far more common than legitimate ones, as was the trickery they used to make it appear to their clients that ghosts of deceased relatives were moving objects in the darkened room of seances. The word telekinesis began to be associated with hoaxes and chicanery.

Despite the frauds, there was a growing interest among the public in paranormal abilities, and telekinesis in particular. It was as if some awareness of the true nature of human beings was welling up inside of people, insisting upon being revealed.

The Other Name

Due to the somewhat sullied history of the telekinesis label new terminology was sought to distinguish serious paranormal study from association with the old term. The more modern name for this ability is Psychokinesis and came to include many paranormal abilities not confined to the simple, original definition of telekinesis.

I've never liked the appellation Psychokinesis, though I can understand its appeal and more correct accounting of the various phenomena in modern thinking. My main objection is to the preface psycho. This is a common term modern slang uses to malign someone as crazy, despite the fact that *psycho* is derived from the Greek word *psukhē*, meaning spirit or breath. Psychic abilities get derided enough without adding fuel to the fire with words that can be used to insinuate people that believe in them are a few connections short upstairs.

By the start of World War I, the term psychokinesis began to come into vogue as an alternative to telekinesis and a way to separate the methods of fake mediums from the investigations and experimentation of people seriously interested in discovering and exploring true paranormal abilities.

The big basket of psychokinesis came to mean: the ability of the mind affecting anything. Of course this included moving objects, but also added in feats such as slowing or speeding up a watch, energy healing of biological tissue, magnetism, shape-shifting, levitation, teleportation, influencing a random number generator, softening metals, transmutation of matter, and control of light. It is even applied in reverse, which is called "binding" and refers to the ability to prevent an object, even a feather-weight one like a pencil, from being moved.

TELEKINESIS

IT'S NOT JUST A MIND POWER

Even the most ardent proponents of psychic and paranormal gifts seem to universally classify telekinesis and the myriad of other psychokinetic abilities, as a power of the mind. While I agree that the mind plays an instigating and focusing role, I believe the actual force that physically moves and affects objects is amplified energy of a person's auric field. Understand and learn to control your personal aura and you open the door to being able to manifest and control a wide range of psychic and paranormal abilities.

TELEKINESIS

HISTORICAL REFERENCES

Despite its detractors, telekinesis has numerous historical references, including in the Bible. In Acts 16:19-40, Paul and Silas were imprisoned in Ephesus, which is located on the coast of modern-day Turkey. They prayed and sang together and at midnight their shackles unlocked and fell to the ground and the heavy door of their prison swung wide open for their escape. Although this may be attributed to divine intervention, it just as easily could have been achieved by Paul and Silas using their own telekinetic power, which they amplified and focused with their prayers and songs.

Fast forwarding to modern times, if you think about fantasy shows like Harry Potter movies or the TV show Charmed; telekinesis, the ability to move and manipulate objects with the strength of your mind or auric field, is one of the most fascinating and desired paranormal powers. Perhaps the greatest real life example of astounding telekinesis power, and likely the inspiration for many modern depictions, is the account of Miriam (Mary Magdalene) saving

Salome in the Oracles of Celestine Light: Vivus, Chapter 58. It was dramatized in Labyrinth of Immortality. Here's a short excerpt:

"We quickly ran over to the edge of the embankment and were horrified to see seven men wading across from the far side of the river and heading straight for our wives! Immediately, we made to launch ourselves down to the river to defend our loved ones.

"But Yeshua held up his arms and asked us to remain where we were. 'It is in times of greatest challenge that the true person of light and power can emerge from within the shell in which they are usually held by everyday life,' he said. 'Let us watch for a moment to see if Miriam discovers who she really is.'

"It was very, very difficult to stand there and watch the scene unfolding below." Yohanan lamented. "I confess that I had a moment of doubt and even anger that Yeshua was restraining us. I was thinking, 'what could Miriam possibly do'?

"Up until that fateful day I never really thought of Miriam as being any different than any of the other apostles, other than she was a woman and Yeshua's wife. Yeshua obviously knew a lot more about her potential than we did. If he was confident enough in Miriam to not intervene in the situation below on the river, then I realized I needed to have faith in him and calm my doubting anxieties.

"*Standing on the raised road, we were not that far away from the river. We could see the men wading across and hear them as they were yelling demeaning slurs at our wives bathing in the river. They were obviously very drunk. Miriam told us later that she thought their behavior was so demented that they must be possessed of devils. We saw her lift her hand up toward them and heard her say forcefully, 'In the name of Elohim, I command the devils within you to depart!'*

"*But her words of banishment to the devils had no effect. The men just laughed and kept coming across the river. Miriam was standing near the middle of the river. Our wives had already waded to the shallows or on to the shore. Salome was quickly moving through the water toward the beach thinking Miriam was right behind her. But when she heard Miriam command the devils to depart she realized she was still standing in the river and she turned back to go and be with her.*

"*Now it was Miriam, who had her back to our shore and was facing the men coming from the far shore, that did not know that Salome was returning to be by her side. The men were almost to Miriam, but she seemed to be in a daze. She told us later it was true, and that she was almost no longer cognizant of the men as she was trying to understand why she had been unable to banish the devils.*

"Her disconnect from the moment was shattered when she heard Salome scream just a few feet away from her as two of the men grabbed her and made to drag her back across the river. Then a very scary thing happened.

Cephas nodded in agreement. "Until that moment, all we had ever seen from Yeshua were miracles of Celestine Light that were peaceful and healing. We actually did not know there was any other kind of Celestine power. I am not overstating or exaggerating to say that except for Yeshua we were all stunned by what happened next." Cephas rolled his hand at Yohanan, indicating he should continue telling the story.

"We saw Miriam turn quickly to face the men that were molesting her beloved Salome. She did not speak a word, but thrust her right hand forward very forcefully. Her fingers were spread wide and turned up. Immediately the men holding Salome let go of her arms as if they were burning logs. They slapped both hands upon their eyes and screamed in agony as they fell into the water."

"We could feel Miriam's fury." Cephas interjected. "It was a palatable energy that touched our auras. I felt a cold shiver of primal fear pass through me."

"I too felt it." Yohanan added. "If we who were her brethren felt the fear, think of the terror those men must have felt."

Yohanan continued his account. "Without giving the men wallowing in agony in the water another thought, Miriam swirled around in her fury to engage the other five assailants. She thrust her arms forward forcefully one after the other, with her fingers turned up and spread wide as she had with the two men she blinded. With every thrust of her arm one of the men lifted out of the water and flew backward through the air. Right thrust, left thrust, right again, until all five men were hurled violently to the other side of the river. They landed with bone-crushing impact on the rocks and in the trees on the far side."

"If you could have seen us up on the road, it would have been quite a sight." Cephas said chuckling in recollection. "I am sure all of our mouths were agape and hanging down as far as they could go. What we had just witnessed Miriam do was completely beyond our comprehension of what was possible."

"I looked down at our wives on the river bank." Yohanan added. "They were huddled together holding on to each other closely, staring at Miriam. They should be grateful that she had saved them, but they were obviously still in shock and fear, not about the men, but about Miriam!"

TELEKINESIS

TELEPORTATION

Having grown up with science fiction shows like Star Trek I always envisioned teleportation to be similar to using the transporter on the starship Enterprise to move from one place to another. The reality and the means by which teleportation occurs are quite different. And as I discovered, it is actually a manifestation of telekinesis. It has happened to me twice. Once to my physical body and once to an object. In both cases the teleporting action was a complete surprise and not something I intentionally initiated.

How Did I Get Here?

The first instance occurred in 1998, when I was living in Ashland, Oregon. I became very upset with something one of my family members did and left the house in a huff to go on a walk and cool off before I said or did something I would later regret. I had walked about two blocks away from our house and toward the outskirts of town, when suddenly my aura started spontaneously expanding at a very rapid rate. In moments I lost conscious awareness of my surroundings. I couldn't tell you if I was standing up, laying down, or still walking during that time. But the marvels were just beginning.

Without warning or prelude, my mind began to receive an astounding stream of knowledge. Understanding and comprehending everything from astrophysics, to all forms of alien life in the universe, to how to take apart and reassemble a nuclear bomb, came pouring into my brain at a ferociously rapid clip. In what seemed to me to be mere moments I felt I had acquired all knowledge on all subjects, and that there was not one single piece of knowledge in existence that did not for that moment in time reside in my head. I should mention here that not only was I not stoned, but in my entire life I have never used any kind of mind or mood altering drug, not even marijuana.

Once my brain was full I came back into an awareness of my surroundings. But I was in the wrong place! I had been walking out of town, but now found myself in the very center of town near the entrance to the movie theater. All the knowledge I had acquired was still in my head but to my great dismay it was draining away rapidly. I could feel it, even see it leaving. Facts I knew with certainty vanished and left me ignorant in just a blink of an eye. But there was still so much new knowledge overflowing inside of me that I was ecstatic and very excited to share it with my family. How I got to the theater had no interest to me at the moment.

I raced home, literally running, because with every stride more of my newly acquired knowledge was vanishing. About 5 minutes after leaving the theater and 10 minutes after originally leaving the house I was back home. Just in that short 5 minutes after becoming aware of my surroundings at the theater, almost all of my newly acquired knowledge had vanished. I desperately tried to hold onto the memories of some of the things I knew would be of interest to my family.

Coming home through the door everyone wanted to give me solace thinking I was still upset because of the original reason I had walked out. I could have cared less about that. I quickly just began to share what had happened to me and the remnants of valuable information that still remained with me that I had gained.

It was only later when we were all reflecting upon the adventure that my wife asked how I had come to be at the theater when I had been walking in the opposite direction heading out of town. I pointed out that I had run home in 5 minutes, but we realized that had been downhill and I wouldn't have been able to run and make the same time going the other direction, even if I had headed for the theater directly from the house instead of walking out of town. It seemed to dawn on all of us at the same time: I had somehow been teleported. It took me many years to understand how.

Mechanics Of Teleportation

It wasn't like the transporter in Star Trek. My atoms didn't dissolve, then get reassembled at the theater. Teleportation more closely follows the laws of physics and Einsteins theories of relativity. Einstein theorized that space itself could be bent. In his case, he imagined gravity as the force that would bend space. I came to realize so could the power of telekinesis, even when it was not consciously applied.

Imagine a piece of paper. In one corner is a dot, point A. In the opposite corner, as far away from point A as you can be on that piece of paper is another dot, point B. If you want to connect in the shortest distance between point A and point B, you need to travel in a long, perfectly straight line across the paper, right? Wrong. If you curve the paper you can bring the two points together so the two corners are touching each other. Now the two points are as one. This is the concept behind wormholes in space that theoretically would connect two points that under normal circumstances would be too distant from one another to travel to. It is the same method, on a much smaller scale that I transported from out of town, to the center of town in the blink of an eye on that fateful day in 1998.

PILOT ROCK UNVEILS POSITIVE ENERGY VORTEX

Pilot Rock

Another of the more amazing experiences I have had, and one also experiencing teleportation, occurred on a beautiful spring day when my wife Sumara and I went for a hike up to Pilot Rock, on the Oregon-California border, to visit two Positive Energy Vortexes and two Dimensional Doorways we had located remotely and now wanted to pinpoint.

It was early May and this was our first hike of the year since the snows had receded and the trails were clear. The combination of amazing scenic views and the opportunity to discover four powerful paranormal energy locations made it a trip we were really looking forward to.

Pilot Rock, as its name implies has been a guidepost for north-south travelers since pioneer days and certainly by Native Americans before that. Strategically located very close to the Siskiyou Pass, right on the border of Oregon and California.

The rock is a columnar basalt monolith, the remnants of an ancient volcano. When you are standing on the rock you are actually standing inside an old volcano. This was the throat of the volcano, where the magma and ash rose up and were blasted out. When the volcano was young it had the familiar conical shaped slopes of a volcano that you see with Mt. Shasta or Black Butte. However, the flanks of the volcano were of softer material and over the years they eroded away leaving only the hard basalt magma throat still standing in what is today Pilot Rock.

On the day of our fateful hike, the days were getting longer so we were not in a hurry to get going and did not arrive in the vicinity of Pilot Rock until around 2:00 in the afternoon. After leaving the highway, we drove a couple of miles on a very rough, unimproved dirt road to reach the parking area at an old quarry. We left the parking area, about 1 mile below the base of Pilot Rock, and began an easy ascent up toward the base of the monolith. The entire monolithic rock is engulfed in a big and powerful Positive Energy Vortex that extends outward at least 50 feet from the base. The most intense energy concentration is at the very top of the monolith. The rush of energy at the top is astounding, but care has to be taken not to let the swirling vortex energy move you right off the edge, as it's a vertical drop down for almost 600 feet and there's not a lot of room at the pointy top of the rock!

We had only walked about 100 feet from the car when Sumara asked if she could borrow the carabineer that I carried my keys on so she could hook her water bottle onto her belt loop and not have to carry it. I unzipped the coat pocket that my keys were in, removed the carabineer and handed it to her, then put my keys back in my jacket pocket and zipped it up to insure they didn't fall out on our hike.

We decided to save the ascent of Pilot Rock for later in the day and first look for an ancient Dimensional Doorway just a short hike down the Pacific Crest Trail (PCT), which intersected the lower portion of the Pilot Rock trail. After a short distance, while seeking the dimensional energy disruption, we located it in a small, well hidden cave, less than 100 feet off the PCT. Though the view of snow-capped Mt. McLoughlin from the location was beautiful, the energy at the doorway was somewhat dark. It was obvious this was a passage that had not been opened for a very long time.

We lingered but a few minutes, then turned our sights toward the monolith. We needed to return the way we came to get back on the trail leading up to Pilot Rock. But I had the not too brilliant idea to take a shortcut and bushwhack straight up the slope above us, assuming we could intersect the Pilot Rock trail at some point. So off we went through the bush. It ended up being a lot more challenging than I had anticipated. The slope was quite steep with many spots of loose, pebbly talus where it was all we could do to not slip and slide down the mountain. Whenever we did reach a substantial bushy area where we had firm footing, we needed to be very careful about what bushes we touched or even allowed to brush against our clothes, as Poison Oak was everywhere!

Finally, after a lot more effort than a shortcut warranted, we intersected the Pilot Rock trail and headed up toward the monolith. The trail up from that point was very steep, dry and dusty, with numerous loose pebbles constantly underfoot making traction treacherous. It was a relief to finally reach the base of the rock itself and have firm footing. The climb up the rock is through a narrow fault fracture that splits the monolith. Other than two 10 foot vertical spots with little for handholds, the 600 foot hand and foot scramble from the base was fairly easy. From the summit, the 360 degree view was one of the most memorable I have ever seen. Majestic Mt. Shasta towered over 14,000 feet due south and the valley in between, over 2000 feet below, took your breath away with its spectacular beauty. Standing within the very center of the Positive Energy Vortex, right at the peak of the monolith, was also an unforgettable experience.

Coming down was fairly easy, but by the bottom of the hill we were looking forward to getting home and taking a nice hot shower, eating a delicious meal and a getting a really sound night's sleep. But the day was not over and our most interesting adventure of the trip was just about to begin.

Out of habit, I reached into my right pants pocket to get my keys to open the Jeep, but they weren't there. Just a little worried, I tried my other pants pocket without success. Then I recollected the history of the keys during our travels that day. After giving Sumara the carabineer for her water bottle at the beginning of our trek, I zipped my keys into a pocket of the light jacket I was wearing.

Before we reached the PCT the day had warmed up and I had taken my jacket off and tied it around my waist. When we were passing through a shady area beneath some large pine trees, Sumara had asked to wear my jacket as she was getting a little chilled. I passed it to her and over the next several hours the jacket went back and forth between us multiple times depending upon who was cold or hot. Most of the afternoon we were in the sun ascending Pilot Rock and the jacket was tied around my waist. On the way back down, once we were back under the forest canopy and the air was cooler, I put it back on.

Happily remembering that my keys were inside my jacket pocket I reached in to get them so we could be on our way. However, they were not in the right pocket, which I was dismayed to find was no longer zipped shut. A serious rush of worry flashed over me as I reached into my left pocket, the only remaining pocket. I looked at Sumara sheepishly, because the keys were not in the left pocket either. Worse, both pocket zippers were open. It became instantly obvious that in passing the jacket back and forth through the day, sometimes wearing it and sometimes tying it around my waist, the zipper had worked open and the keys had fallen out.

I apologized to Sumara. Though I knew she was looking forward to the comforts of home, I told her we were going to need to retrace our steps until we found the keys. I was pretty sure we would find them quickly on the old dirt road that led from the parking area to the Pilot Rock Trail. It was on the road that we had the most movement of the jacket, both going up and coming down.

Before we left to look for the keys we said a short prayer, then began retracing our steps. Spaced out on either side of the road we walked slowly, scanning the ground for the keys. If they still had the bright red carabineer attached that I had given Sumara for her water bottle they would have been easy to spot. But without that, their mostly dull bronze color was going to be a challenge to spot on the rocky, road.

We reached the trail head for Pilot Rock without finding the keys. It was getting late, but I realized we would need to backtrack our entire hike of the day until we found the keys. We were the only ones up in the area, a part of the Siskiyou Wilderness, and it was a long walk back home. Resolute, we retraced our steps back to the first dimensional doorway. On the trail under the forest canopy it was much darker and we really had to walk slow and bend down as close as we could to scan for the keys. Unfortunately, after looking just as hard on the way back, we still came up empty-handed.

Now the really daunting challenge was before us. We needed to retrace our steps up the Pilot Rock trail and if necessary scale the monolith again. There was no way we could backtrack through the area we had bushwhacked a shortcut, so we just had to hope the keys had not fallen out there and put all of our focus on the Pilot Rock ascent.

Climbing up the steep talus slope of the Pilot Rock trail was tiring for both of us. One trip like that in a day was great; two trips, not so great. But we had to go on until it was dark. We didn't feel we had a choice. We had our cell phone, but there was no reception in our remote area, even if there had been anyone to call for assistance.

By the time we neared the base of Pilot Rock Sumara said she was sorry, but she just couldn't take one more step up. I told her to wait for me and I would climb the monolith again by myself. About a half hour later, I met up with her at the same spot I had left her, but once again, with no keys to show for my effort.

We still had hope and carefully scrutinizing the ground we had already traversed going up, we slowly, on increasingly overworked, wobbly legs, made our way back down. When we arrived at the Jeep again it was almost dark and getting colder. I pulled out my wallet where luckily I was smart enough to keep a spare key to open the door. On Jeeps, the key that opens the door is normally the same key that starts the ignition, but a couple of years earlier I had to rekey the ignition when it broke. So now I needed two keys: the old one for the door and the new one for the ignition. Unfortunately, I only had a spare door key.

The first thing we did after getting in the Jeep was to buoy our spirits with one of Sumara's famous raw desserts, which we had stashed in the car as a rewarding treat to share at the conclusion of our hike. It melted in our mouths as we discussed the options for getting out of our predicament. While we were talking, Sumara completely forgetting our predicament for a moment, reached over to where the keys should be hanging from the steering column ignition, to flip them on to see what time it was on the digital clock. She pulled back her hand in disappointment when it reached the empty space where the keys should be dangling, because of course there were no keys there.

We wondered what we were going to do. If our phone worked I could at the very least call a tow truck to come and get us. I let out a sigh thinking about the hike I was going to need to take on the very rocky, unimproved road, hungry, in the dark, for two miles, to get close enough to the highway to get cell reception. I put my head down and cradled it in my hand as I contemplated one more effort my exhausted body was going to need to endure. Moving my hand off my forehead, I was staring right at the empty spot on the steering column where the keys belonged. To my utter amazement, they were swinging slowly back and forth in the ignition, motivated by some unseen force! I quickly looked over at Sumara and pointed at the swinging keys. We were both shocked and incredulous. We realized something momentous had just happened.

At first glance it would seem that this account would be better labeled as Divine Intervention, and we certainly did give our thanks to God after the keys appeared. But the more I thought about it, the more I realized finding the keys back where they belonged, was not a gift from God. The gift from God was our paranormal powers, which God gave us, to bend space and teleport the keys from wherever they had fallen on the mountain, back into the Jeep when we needed them most.

Whether we did it or God did it, one way or the other the keys were teleported. I believe it was us, and that this is God's true gift of love to all of us: not to answer our prayers by doing things for us, but gifting us upon our creation with great paranormal abilities to work our own miracles, if we are willing to live in the light and discover and embrace our power.

Most psychic and paranormal gifts work easier and more powerfully when they are exercised with focus and passion. This is especially true with the greater powers. In our quest to find our missing keys, we had total focus and an escalating passion to discover them before the darkness of the night overtook us.

An interesting twist worth noting is what we were focused upon. Like the day I physically teleported from outside of town to the theater at the center of town, the thought of teleporting our keys sadly never entered our minds. Instead we trekked off like a couple of Mundanes to find them searching with our eyes. Nevertheless, once we had backtracked our hike and returned to the Jeep empty-handed, teleportation was the only viable means for us to have the keys when we needed them. Unconsciously we called upon a hidden paranormal power.

Though we were at a loss as to "how," when we sat in our Jeep contemplating a plan to get home, we were at our peak passion and focus of wanting to find our keys. And Voila! They appeared. Though we didn't focus on teleporting them, our passion and desire to have them manifested them for us, as that was the power which provided the most viable way to achieve our goal. It was the instinctual action necessary to produce the required result; little different than unconsciously moving your hand rapidly up to catch an object flying at you unexpectedly. Only this unconscious action gave us an inspiring and motivating glimpse of the vast potential that slumbers inside of us, waiting for us to awaken and call it out.

TELEKINESIS

EXPERIMENTS WITH TELEKINESIS

I have had good success with several experiments. Some are shared below and I encourage you to try them by practicing them at home. If done under controlled conditions to ensure your breath or movement are not affecting the test object, they are a great way to help you realize you have this potent ability and exercise your mind and aura to increase its power. I know I am!

College Experiment (Telekinesis Exercise # 1)

My first exposure to actual telekinesis was of all places, in a college physics class as a Freshman. I think as a joke, a means to lighten up a serious class, the professor asked us if anyone believed in the psychic power of telekinesis. Because it was a science class and that was considered a fake pseudoscience, most people chuckled and no one but me was foolish enough to raise their hand. As I was the only one imprudent enough to admit belief in a non-science, the professor with a condescending smile on his face, gave me the opportunity to design an experiment that the entire class could participate in, limited to 5 minutes, to test whether an object could be caused to move without physical touching, or any obvious physical motivating force. For telekinesis to be a viable possibility, there could not be any other more likely cause.

Embarrassed with a beet red flushed face, but thinking quickly, wishing I hadn't raised my hand and certain I was going to be made to look like a fool, I split the class in two and had them stand in a group on opposite sides of a large wooden table, about 10' x 5', we used for big experiments. Half the class stood on one side and the other on the opposite side. There was a 1 foot gap left between students and the table to insure nobody touched it. No active participants stood on the ends, but I asked two students to stand on the ends to monitor each side to insure the table remained untouched.

I placed a single pencil right in the middle of the table parallel to the long side, equally between the two sides of students. The experiment was to see if either side could move the pencil even a little bit. I hoped that the competitive team spirit would heighten any psychic abilities and be more likely to manifest a reaction. Plus, everyone focused on the same task, should amplify any telekinetic power.

After 4 minutes absolutely nothing had happened. Entering the last minute allotted for the experiment, it wasn't looking promising. Suddenly the pencil started to slowly roll toward one side of the table! It was moving at a steady, undeniable clip and nobody was moving or blowing it! After it had rolled about 2 feet and was getting close to the edge, it started to slowly and jerkily spin around in place. That lasted for about 5 seconds and then it began to roll slowly toward the other side!

As it neared the opposite side it suddenly stopped just before it fell off the edge. After about 10 seconds the pencil started rolling again in fits and starts, back in the other direction. When it was in the center of the table the 5 minute buzzer went off and the experiment ended. With a big laugh and a clap of his hands the professor called it a draw.

Most people were trying to act cool, like it was no big deal, just another science experiment where what we thought happened, obviously did not happen as it appeared and more facts needed to be gleaned to make a conclusion. Several were dismissive claiming there had to be a trick employed that we were unaware of. The professors light hearted response at the end of the experiment subtly encouraged both of those reactions.

But there were a few students expressing amazement in wide-eyed wonder, including me. I couldn't think of any other explanation except telekinesis. In truth, I wasn't reacting much like a scientist who wouldn't think of drawing conclusions without several intensive tests. I was more like someone who wanted to believe the unbelievable. But then, my life had always been full of the inexplicable and implausible, so I was more open to the possibility.

The professor asked the class to propose possible motivating forces other than telekinesis, but not one person came up with any theories that weren't even more far-fetched. It was left as a test needing further experimenting to determine the motivating force, but we never revisited the subject and most people continued to think it had just been some type of prank. However, I did get extra points for designing a good experiment on a moment's notice.

The Science Behind Telekinesis

Telekinesis is certainly one of the more dramatic and magical appearing paranormal powers. You'll have a challenge convincing many people that see it in action, that it's not magic. The reality is, it is a biological and/or electromagnetic manifestation of the *First Law of Thermodynamics*, a law of physics, as are many other paranormal powers. Understanding this aspect helps me to get more excited and confident in achieving results.

Stated simply, the first law of Thermodynamics establishes that energy cannot be created or destroyed. ***But it can be changed from one form of energy into another, or transferred from one storage vessel to another.*** Heat, light, magnetism, chemical, kinetic, and electrical are all forms of energy that can be transferred or changed.

Most of the energy we receive as humans comes from the food we eat. Food energy is a chemical form of energy and is measured in calories. Our bodies only use about 40% of the energy taken in by eating food to maintain the body systems. The other 60% is available to be changed into another form of energy and used for work or transferred to something or someone else.

For instance, when you exercise, you are changing the chemical energy stored in your body into kinetic (motion) energy. When you do an energy or spiritual healing of someone that is sick, you are transferring multiple forms of energy from you to them, and channeling energy from beyond yourself as well. The energy transfer enters into them revitalizing and repairing their ailing body.

How You Can Practice And Expand Your Telekinetic Ability

In addition to doing your own variety of the pencil experiment from my college physics class, (remember the more people, the more powerful) here are some additional exercises that I enjoy and have found helpful. Be patient and practice regularly to discover and increase your own telekinetic ability.

I encourage you to begin with very light objects. The less dense an object is, the more space there is between molecules. That creates more surface area for you to more easily affect the object with telekinesis.

Telekinesis is one of those paranormal abilities greatly enhanced by focus and concentration. Spoon bending, a form of telekinesis, is an exception, as it works best if you are unfocused.

Remember, you are creating a beam of energy between you and the object. The object is moved by the auric force you exert by the focused thought you apply to it. If you are doing it correctly you will have distinct and unusual physical sensations deep in your body as your auric field coalesces ready to burst forth in a concentrated beam of power.

The required focus is no different than if you were shooting an arrow at a distant target. If you didn't focus on the bulls-eye and concentrate on taking careful aim, but instead pulled your bow back and shot your arrow while admiring the clouds in the sky, it is highly unlikely your arrow would impact the target. It is the same with the telekinetic beam of auric energy you are sending. It must have a target and you must have focus and concentration to hit and affect the target.

TELEKINESIS EXERCISE # 2

This exercise will be conducted with what is known as a *PSI Wheel.* You can easily make one at home from a sheet of paper or a piece of aluminum foil. Or, if you prefer, you can buy one from many metaphysical stores.

If you would like to build your own, you'll just need 3 items: a 2 inch long sewing needle, a 2x2 inch square of typing paper or foil, and a small piece of clay or a cork 1-1½ inches in diameter.

1. Cut the paper into a 2-3 inch square; or you can use a 3x3 inch *Post It* note.

2. Fold the square of paper in half, creating a rectangle and a strong crease line.

3. Unfold the paper, but not so much that you press the crease out. Now fold it in half the opposite direction. You should end up with a cross shape pattern formed by the creases.

4. Now make a diagonal fold through the cross pattern. You are folding the paper into a triangle.

5. Make one more diagonal fold of a diagonal from the other side.

6. Unfold your folded paper. You should have a square showing four crease lines, equal distance apart, creating 8 end points at the edge of the paper.

7. The next two steps create the 3 dimensional PSI Wheel. Hold the paper so one of the long crease lines that goes from one side of the paper to the other is sandwiched between your thumb and forefinger, with one hand sandwiching the crease on one side of the paper and the other hand sandwiching the crease on the other side. Now gently press the thumb and forefingers toward each other and simultaneously press the

two hands on opposite sides towards each other.

8. Repeat this for the other linear crease. As you do so, you can alternate back and forth to the other crease and form your paper into a 3 dimensional PSI Wheel. You should end up with a paper with a sharp center point and four slightly angled vanes.

9. Make a small ball of clay and stick the needle upright into the clay with the pointy end up.

10. Gently set your PSI Wheel on top of the needle tip with an even balance. It is now ready for you to move it with the power of your auric field.

11. Sit in a chair at a table with the PSI Wheel on the table in front of you. Place your hands on either side of the PSI Wheel, 6-12 inches apart, palms facing each other.

12. Envision a spinning ball of energy swirling between your hands. Very quickly the PSI Wheel should begin to move. It may vacillate directions for a moment, then continuously begin spinning in one direction. And it may speed up considerably.

Advanced Practice

Find a glass bowl, a bell jar, or a sufficiently large glass that you can put over the PSI Wheel to insure there are no breezes from breathing or movement, or hot air emanating from your hands, that could be affecting the PSI Wheel. Place your hands on either side, without touching the glass and move the PSI Wheel with your auric field.

More Advanced Practice

Sit back 3 to 6 feet from the PSI Wheel still under a glass. Hold up your right hand with your palm facing the PSI Wheel but at least 3 feet away. Swirl and concentrate your auric energy inside of you, then shoot it down your arm, out your hand and move the PSI Wheel with the stream of force.

Even More Advanced Practice

Sit back at least 6 feet from the PSI Wheel still under a glass. Keep your hands at your side. Swirl and concentrate your auric energy inside of you, then focus it purely through the intention of your mind and move the PSI Wheel with the stream of force. Hint: Imagine yourself *one* with the PSI Wheel. The molecules that form the PSI Wheel are part of the molecules that form your body. The PSI Wheel is as much an extension of you as your finger. Just like your finger, you can move it anytime you will it to be so.

TELEKINESIS

TELEKINESIS EXERCISE # 3

In this exercise you will move a toothpick floating on water.

1. Set up the toothpick floating in a bowl of water on a table.

2. Sit nearby in a comfortable chair. Be sure not to touch the table with any part of your body during the exercise. Allow the water to become perfectly still and calm before you begin moving the toothpick.

3. Swirl and concentrate your auric energy inside of you, then focus it purely through the intention of your mind and move the toothpick with the stream of force. *Hint:* Imagine yourself *one* with the toothpick. The molecules that form the toothpick are part of the molecules that form your body. The toothpick is as much of an extension of you as your finger is. Just like your finger, you can move it anytime you will it to be so.

4. Once you have movement of the toothpick, focus on controlling the movement by willing it to move to the right, then to the left, then forward, then backwards.

Advanced practice:

To insure there are no breezes, heat emanations, or table movements affecting the toothpick, place it in the bowl with the water and toothpick underneath a larger bowl turned upside down.

TELEKINESIS EXERCISE # 4

In this advanced exercise you will float a feather. Take a clean dry jar with a lid and place a feather inside. It should be a good size but still small enough that it does not touch any sides of the jar. Smaller feathers are OK as well.

1. Seal the lid on the jar with the feather inside.

2. Set the jar on a table and sit nearby in a comfortable chair. Be sure not to touch the table in any way.

3. Swirl and concentrate your auric energy inside of you, then focus it purely through the intention of your mind and move the feather with the stream of force. **Hint:** Imagine yourself *one* with the feather. The molecules that form the feather are part of the molecules that form your body. The feather is as much of an extension of you as your finger is. Just like your finger you can move it anytime you will it to be so.

4. Move the feather. Once you have movement,

lift the feather up so it is floating free inside the sealed jar.

5. Once the feather is freely floating, focus on moving it up and down and side to side as you will it to be so, rather than just aimlessly moving around inside the jar.

TELEKINESIS EXERCISE # 5

In this exercise you will learn to control fire. Controlling fire is one of the more exciting aspects of telekinesis and this experiment is just the beginning of what you can do.

1. Light a candle of ½-1 inch in diameter, that stands 6-12 inches tall and set it on a table.

2. Remove all distractions from the room. You should be alone and insure that you will be undisturbed.

3. Sit down comfortably about 2 feet from the candle, far enough away that neither your breath nor any slight movement will reach and move the flame.

4. Look closely at the flame; notice the different parts, colors and translucencies.

5. Observe the tip and how it tapers and undulates.

6. Become one with the flame. Encompass it in your aura. Though you are too far away to

physically feel its warmth, feel it with your aura.

7. Now focus on bending the flame in one direction or other; not just flickering, which is a movement that could be caused by a passing movement of air from any source. This is a focus to physically bend the flame at a sharp angle and keep it bent for a period of time far longer than a flicker.

8. You may be helped by holding up one or both hands with palms facing the candle and sending a concentrated beam of your aura through your hands at the flame.

Advanced practice

Conduct the same exercise but eliminate any possibility of your breath or movement affecting the flame by putting the candle inside a glass cylinder with an open top for the smoke to vent.

More advanced practice

With the candle still inside the glass cylinder, sit in a comfortable chair far enough away from the table that you cannot touch it with any part of your body. Swirl and concentrate your auric energy inside of you, then focus it purely through the intention of your mind and bend the flame with the stream of force. *Hint:* Imagine yourself *one* with the flame. The molecules that form the flame are part of the molecules that form your body. The flame is as much of an extension of you as your finger is; just like your finger you can move it or bend it anytime you will it to be so.

TELEKINESIS

FOCUS EXERCISE #1
The Half Dollar Flip

1. For this exercise you will need a United States Kennedy 50 cent coin. This coin is used because it has a very memorable image on the reverse side. If you are in another country, obtain the largest or most distinctive coin issued in your country. You are not going to use the side with a face of an ex-president or ruler. You want a coin with a striking image on the reverse side.

2. Once you have your coin go to http://www. random.org/coins/. This an excellent Random Number Generator.

3. Select the coin from their list that you are holding.

4. Enter **1** in the flip box. You are going to make *tails* come up, one flip at a time.

5. Click *Flip Coin(s)*.

6. An image of the coin you flipped will appear. It may show heads or it may show tails. If it

shows heads, flip it again until the image on your computer is tails, which should match the coin you are holding in your hand.

7. Now you are ready to begin the exercise. Look at the coin in your hand. Focus on the image on the reverse side. Look at it in detail in all parts. Think *tails* in your mind or even say it aloud.

8. Click the button on the website that says *Flip Again.* The image will come up with your coin, either *heads* or *tails.*

9. Focus once more on the image of the coin in your hand. You are only using the reverse side of the coin. You will be choosing *tails* 100% of the time. Never alternate and choose *heads.*

10. When you have focused strongly, and stated *tails* aloud or in your mind, click *Flip Again.*

11. Once more the site will show you *heads* or *tails.* Continue to focus on tails and flipping the coin.

12. Keep a mental or written record of the number of times tails comes up compared to the total number of flips.

The Law of Averages predicts you will have 50% tails and 50% heads. I tried this just flipping a coin without thinking about which side would show and it came up exactly 50 heads and 50 tails after 100 flips. In a short run of 10-20 flips, this average may be off a bit. But if 100 flips were done at random, with no focus on *heads* or *tails*, it will come up 50-50 nearly every time with only tiny deviation. Therefore, any substantial deviation that you create by focusing on just tails is quite significant. By focusing only on the task at hand, stating your intention aloud or in your mind by saying *tails*, and seeing the picture of tails in your mind as you click the *Flip Again* button, you will typically be able to make 60-70 out of 100 tails appear. This is actually quite an astounding feat! The best I have ever done is 79 out of 100.

How Is The Random Number Generator Affected?

How this is being accomplished, by what psychic ability or paranormal power, a Random Number Generator on a computer in some distant, unknown town can be affected, is a curious question.

The most likely source is the paranormal power of **telekinesis**, which allows you to physically control or move an object by the power of your mind and auric energy. Being able to influence a random number generator is often attributed to telekinetic power.

So the coin flip exercise helps you in two ways. It builds up your power of focus and concentration while simultaneously increasing your telekinetic powers.

TELEKINESIS

SPOON BENDING

I'm happy to be able to end this paranormal jaunt with a really fun form of telekinesis -- spoon bending. You may have heard of spoon bending. It was made famous back in the 70's by Israeli psychic, Uri Geller. There is some dispute, even among psychics, as to whether Geller was legitimately bending spoons with psychic powers or merely using magicians tricks. But from my own experience I know that spoon, fork and knife bending is a real phenomenon. I became a big believer when I watched my daughter bend them like they were made of clay when she was only 6 years old, including the stiff tines of forks and the thick bowls of spoons!

The concept behind psychically bending metal utensils is to inject psychic energy by projecting your aura into the utensil until it becomes soft like a stiff Tootsie Roll. At that point you can pretty much bend them into any shape you desire with little effort. Areas on the utensil where it is narrow and thin are easy to bend with just a little physical effort and no psychic energy, so you can't count bends at those locations, unless they include sharp twists. But when you start almost effortlessly bending the rigid tines of forks and the thick bowls of spoons, you know you are doing something supernatural.

How To Use Psychic Energy To Bend Utensils

In 2004, when my youngest daughter Angel was 6 years old, we had read a little about spoon bending parties they were having in San Francisco. My wife Sumara and I decided to give it a try ourselves. We went down to the local Good Will second-hand store and purchased a couple of dozen used forks, knives and spoons from their basket of old utensils. We had a mixture of cheap thin ones and quality thick, heavy ones.

When we got home we first began as is typical with psychic endeavors, by focusing on bending the utensils as we held them in our hands and applied light pressure at various spots. We both succeeded in bending both forks and spoons right at the narrowest part of the neck, but that was it. And we both agreed that was just done using our strength, because it didn't require much. While we were laser beam focused on our psychic task, our 6 year old daughter Angel had picked up a spoon off the pile on the table and was playing with it. Neither of us paid attention to her because we wanted to remain focused on our own spoon bending projects.

After about 5 minutes and a couple of additional sacrificial utensils, neither Sumara or I had any success bending anything more than the narrow neck of the utensils. Taking a break we looked for the first time over at Angel. She was playing with a utensil in her hand and she had 2 laying on the table in front of her that were convoluted like pretzels!

"How did you do that Angel?" I asked curiously with a little awe.

"I don't know," she replied. "I just played with the spoon while I watched TV and it bent."

I had completely forgotten about the TV being on. It was out of my view from where I had been sitting at the table and I had asked Angel to turn off the sound when we began our bending experiments because we didn't want any distractions.

"Did you tell the spoon to bend?" I asked.

"At first," she replied simply.

"Then I forgot about it and just played with it in my hands while I watched TV. I thought you were bending them too." She said, seemingly perplexed as to why I was asking her about something she thought I had also been doing.

"Yeah, we were." I acknowledged. Just not with as much success as you had."

Then it dawned on me. Perhaps spoon bending was an anomaly in the realm of psychic powers. Instead of requiring focus, maybe it needed disinterest. That was a fairly radical thought in my mind, but the would-be scientist in me decided it would only be fair to test the theory. So we turned up the volume and all of us watched TV while we "played" with another round of utensils. Like Angel had taught us, we did command them to "bend" before we forgot about them and began watching TV.

The results were beyond our expectations. The utensils bent so easily after just a couple of minutes that we could literally manipulate them into any shape we desired. It became a friendly challenge to see who could bend their utensil into the most interesting piece of art. Angel won every time. It was amazing all the twists, turns and bends she could make the thickest points of the utensils contort into.

We also discovered in later experiments that you do not need to watch TV. ***The simple key is disinterest.*** We could sit and chat about school, or where we were going on our next hike, or relive our last adventure. The more disinterest we had, the easier the utensil ended up bending. The only other key was to focus for a brief moment right at the beginning, ***before becoming disinterested***, and command the utensil to "bend."

IN CONCLUSION

Telekinesis is such a fascinating psychic/ paranormal ability. I hope you have as much pleasure and fulfillment discovering and using it as I have had over the years. Just remember, the secret is practice; not just telekinesis practice, but everyday in many ways exercising all of the psychic and paranormal abilities you are interested in. Even when you are unsure if you have any, or at least have never manifested any, keep practicing the ones that interest you the most. Don't get discouraged if you do not succeed quickly. What I have seen over many years is the trait that separates the psychic achievers from the psychic wannabees is persistence. Persist until you succeed, and you WILL succeed.

Namaste,

Embrosewyn

EMBROSEWYN'S BOOKS

WORDS OF POWER AND TRANSFORMATION
101+ Magickal Words and Sigils of Celestine Light To Manifest Your Desires

Whatever you seek to achieve or change in your life, big or small, Celestine Light magickal words and sigils can help your sincere desires become reality.

Drawing from an ancient well of magickal power, the same divine source used by acclaimed sorcerers, witches and spiritual masters through the ages, the 101+ magickal words and sigils are revealed to the public for the very first time. They can create quick and often profound improvements in your life.

It doesn't matter what religion you follow or what you believe or do not believe. The magickal words and sigils are like mystical keys that open secret doors regardless of who holds the key. If you put the key in and turn it, the door will open and the magick will swirl around you!

From the beginner to the Adept, the Celestine Light words of power and sigils will expand your world and open up possibilities that may have seemed previously unachievable. Everything from something simple like finding a lost object, to something powerful like repelling a psychic or physical attack, to something of need such as greater income, to something life changing like finding your Soul Mate.

Some may wonder how a few spoken words combined with looking for just a moment at a peculiar image could have such immediate and often profound effects. The secret is these are ancient magick words of compelling power and the sigils are the embodiment of their magickal essence. Speaking or even thinking the words, or looking at or even picturing the sigil in your mind, rapidly draws angelic and magickal energies to you like iron to a magnet to fulfill the worthy purpose you desire.

This is a book of potent white magick of the light. Without a lot of training or ritual, it gives you the ability to overcome darkness threatening you from inside or out. For what is darkness except absence of the light? When light shines, darkness fades and disappears, not with a roar, but with a whimper.

Use the words and sigils to call in the magickal energies to transform and improve your life in every aspect. In this comprehensive book you will find activators to propel your personal growth, help you excel in school, succeed in your own business, or launch you to new heights in your profession. It will give you fast acting keys to improve your relationships, change your luck, revitalize your health, and develop and expand your psychic abilities.

Embrosewyn Tazkuvel is an Adept of the highest order in Celestine Light. After six decades of using magick and teaching it to others he is now sharing some of the secrets of what he knows with you. Knowledge that will instantly connect you to divine and powerful universal forces that with harmonic resonance, will unleash the magickal you!

Inside you will discover:

- 101 word combinations that call in magickal forces like a whirlwind of light.
- 177 magickal words in total.
- 101 sigils to go with each magickal word combination to amplify the magickal results you seek.
- 101 audio files you can listen to; helping you have perfect pronunciation of the Words of Power regardless of your native language. Available directly from the eBook and with a link in the paperback edition.

AURAS
How To See, Feel & Know

TOP REVIEWS

#1 Amazon bestseller in multiple categories since 2012. Used as a comprehensive reference book in aura and chakra classes around the world. Filled with real life accounts of Embrosewyns adventures with auras, plus 47 **full color** pictures and illustrations, with 17 dynamic eye exercises to help you rapidly begin to see the beautiful world of auras.

"Mr. Tazkuvel does a wonderful job at making such a complicated and specific subject like auras easy to learn while entertaining the reader with his own experiences as an aura reader throughout his life. The guide is well-written, casual but informative, vivid with imagery (from pictures to illustrations), provides tips/tools for training the mind/eyes and ensures that the reader gets a comprehensive guide to auras in a real and tangible way." ~R. Coker, Amazon Top 1000 Reviewer

"This is one of the most interesting books I have read to date. I had absolutely no idea that I could 'train' myself to see auras! Although I still have a ways to go, I can honestly tell that I am able to pick up on people's auras. The parts on body language and the authors personal story were icing on the cake. Loved it and will definitely be telling everyone I know about it!" ~Momto4BookLover, Amazon Top 2000 Reviewer

"I was a huge skeptic and got the book thinking I was going to blast it in the reviews. After reading through it though I realize that I was completely wrong! The author does a great job explaining exactly what an aura is, as well as how to interpret them. There are

very good exercises to help you train your eyes to see auras." ~Irish Times, Amazon Top 2000 Reviewer

Auras: How to See, Feel & Know, is like three books in one!

- It's an entertaining read as Embrosewyn recalls his early childhood and high school experiences seeing auras, and the often humorous reactions by everyone from his mother to his friends when he told them what he saw.

- It is also a complete training manual to help you quickly be able to see Auras in vibrant color. It includes 17 eye exercises and dozens of Full Color pictures, enabling anyone with vision in both eyes to begin seeing vividly colored auras around any person. The secret is in retraining the focusing parts of your eyes to see things that have always been there, but you have never been able to see before. Auras: How to See, Feel & Know, includes all the power techniques, tools and Full Color eye exercises from Embrosewyn's popular workshops.

- Additionally, there is a fascinating chapter on body language. Embrosewyn teaches in his workshops to not just rely on your interpretation of the aura alone, but to confirm it with another indicator such as body language. Auras: How to See, Feel & Know goes in depth with thorough explanations and great pictures to show you all the common body language indicators used to confirm what someone's aura is showing you.

For those who already have experience seeing auras, the deeper auric layers and subtle auric nuances and the special ways to focus your eyes to see them, are explained in detail, with accompanying Full Color pictures to show you how the deeper layers and auric aberrations appear.

SOUL MATE AURAS
How To Use Your Aura to Find Your Soul Mate

The romantic dream of finding your Soul Mate, the person with whom you resonate on every level of your being, is more than a wishful notion. It is a deeply embedded, primal desire that persists on some level despite what may have been years of quiet, inner frustration and included relationships that while fulfilling on some levels, still fell short of the completeness of a Soul Mate.

Once found, your relationship with your Soul Mate can almost seem like a dream at times. It will be all you expected and probably much more. Having never previously had a relationship that resonated in harmony and expansiveness on every level of your being, you will have had nothing to prepare you for its wonder. Having never stood atop a mountain that tall with an expansiveness so exhilarating, once experienced, a committed relationship with your Soul Mate will give you a bliss and fulfillment such as you probably only imagined in fairy tales.

But how to find your Soul Mate? That is the million dollar question. The vast majority of people believe finding your Soul Mate is like a magnetic attraction, it will somehow just happen; in some manner you'll just be inevitably drawn to each other. The harsh reality is, 99% of people realize by their old age that it never happened. Or, if it did occur they didn't recognize their Soul Mate at the time, because they were looking for a different ideal.

Soul Mate Auras: How to Use Your Aura to Find Your Soul Mate gives you the master keys to unlock the passageway to discovering your Soul Mate using the certainty of your auric connections. Every person has a unique aura and auric field generated by their seven energy centers and their vitality. Find the person that you resonate strongly with on all seven energy centers and you'll find your Soul Mate!

Everyone can sense and see auras. In Soul Mate Auras full color eye and energy exercises will help you learn how to see and feel auras and how to use that ability to identify where in the great big world your Soul Mate is living. Once you are physically in the presence of your prospective Soul Mate, you will know how to use your aura to energetically confirm that they are the one. The same methods can be used to discover multiple people that are Twin Flames with you; not quite seven auric connection Soul Mates, but still deep and expansive connections to you on five to six energy centers.

Soul Mate Auras also includes an in-depth procedure to determine if someone is a Twin Flame or Soul Mate, not by using your aura, but by honestly and rationally evaluating your connections on all seven of your energy centers. This is an invaluable tool for anyone contemplating marriage or entering a long-term committed relationship. It also serves as a useful second opinion confirmation for anyone that has used their aura to find their Soul Mate.

To help inspire and motivate you to create your own "happily ever after," Soul Mate Auras is richly accentuated with dozens of full color photos of loving couples along with profound quotes from famous to anonymous people about the wonder of Soul Mates.

Treat yourself to the reality of finding your Soul Mate or confirming the one that you have already found! Scroll to the upper left of the page and click on Look Inside to find out more about what's inside this book!

Secret Earth Series

INCEPTION
BOOK 1

TOP REVIEWS

"I simply couldn't put it down! It has, in some ways, changed the very way I think. It's exciting, adventurous and keeps you hanging on to the edge of your seat throughout! You don't wanna miss this one!" ~**Barbara Cary, Amazon Top 1000 Reviewer**

"The writing is clear and vivid, both opening doors in readers' imaginations and making heady concepts accessible at the same time." ~**Alex Prosper, Amazon Top 1000 Reviewer**

"What an adventurous and mind-captivating story! I absolutely loved it! If you are like me, you will find yourself not being able to put this book down until it is finished. That's how good it is. I could easily see it being made into a full-scale Hollywood movie." ~**Anna , Amazon Top 5000 Reviewer**

Could it be possible that there is a man alive on the Earth today that has been here for two thousand years? How has he lived so long? And why? What secrets does he know? Can his knowledge save the Earth or is it doomed?

Continuing the epic historical saga begun in the *Oracles of Celestine Light*, but written as a novel rather than a chronicle, Inception unveils the life and adventures of Lazarus of Bethany and his powerful and mysterious sister Miriam of Magdala.

The first book of the Secret Earth series, *Inception*, reveals the hidden beginnings of the strange, secret life of Lazarus. From his comfortable position as the master of caravans to Egypt he is swept into a web of intrigue involving his enigmatic sister Miriam and a myriad of challenging dangers that never seem to end and spans both space and time.

Some say Miriam is an angel, while others are vehement that she is a witch. Lazarus learns the improbable truth about his sister, and along with twenty-three other courageous men and women, is endowed with the secrets of immortality. But he learns that living the secrets is not as easy as knowing them. And living them comes at a price; one that needs to be paid in unwavering courage, stained with blood, built with toil, and endured with millenniums of sacrifice, defending the Earth from all the horrors that might have been. Inception is just the beginning of their odyssey.

DESTINY
Book 2

In preparation, before beginning their training as immortal Guardians of the Earth, Lazarus of Bethany and his wife Hannah were asked to go on a short visit to a world in another dimension. "Just to look around a bit and get a feel for the differences," Lazarus's mysterious sister, Miriam of Magdala assured them.

She neglected to mention the ravenous monstrous birds, the ferocious fire-breathing dragons, the impossibly perfect people with sinister ulterior motives, and the fact that they would end up being naked almost all the time! And that was just the beginning of the challenges!

UNLEASH YOUR PSYCHIC POWERS

TOP REVIEWS

"Along with information on auras, channeling and animal whispering it contains just about every psychic and paranormal topic you can think of. The section on Ki energy was also very good- make that excellent. The author really over delivers in material and it is a nice change from books with hardly any info." ~**Diana L., Amazon Top 500 Reviewer**

"The author shows a skill for weaving words and explaining the intricacies of the wealth of psychic realms, managing to introduce me to all the many psychic areas a person could become proficient in... and then he showed me how to begin my journey of uncovering my own talents in the psychic world. From a reader's standpoint, the book is filled with countless insights into psychic powers/abilities as well as a deeper understanding of how to train your mind/

body to become in tune with the psychic world." ~L. Collins, Amazon Top 1000 Reviewer

"A welcome relief. I was a little skeptical about the validity of the contents of this book . . . UNTIL I read it. Being a paranormal researcher myself, and up-to-date on psychic phenomena, the ins and outs, the dos and don'ts, and all the scams in-between, I was ready for a none too favorable review. How nice to be disappointed! This impressive book is very well written; and remarkably - it is comprehensive without being boring. I strongly suggest that you read it from cover to cover BEFORE delving into the supernatural world of Psychic Power - from Channeling to Psychic Self Defense, and Telepathy to my personal favorite- Lucid Dreams." ~Lyn Murray, Author-Poet Laureate-Artist

A comprehensive guidebook for all levels of practitioners of the psychic and paranormal arts. Each one of the twenty supernatural abilities presented, including Clairvoyance, Animal Whispering, Lucid Dreaming, Precognition, Astral Projection, Channeling, Telekinesis and Telepathy, include easy-to-follow, step-by-step instructions on how you can unleash the full potential of these potent powers in your own life. Spiced with personal stories of Embrosewyn's five decades of experience discovering, developing and using psychic and paranormal talents. Paranormal abilities have saved Embrosewyn's life and the lives of his family members on multiple occasions. Learning to fully develop your own supernatural talents may come in just as handy one day.

PSYCHIC SELF DEFENSE

TOP REVIEW

Regardless of your beliefs, its an elegantly composed and greatly fascinating book. The writer's composing style easy is to follow through. I've read a couple of pages I ended up unable to put the book down. Assuming that you've generally been fascinated about whether psychic capabilities are "genuine" or perhaps that you have some of your own, this is really the book that you need to peruse. ~**Jayden Sanders, Amazon Top 10,000 Reviewer**

Have you ever felt a negative energy come over you for no apparent reason when you are near someone or around certain places? Psychic Self Defense details 17 common psychic threats, with exact, effective counter measures including many real life examples from Embrosewyn's 5 decades of personal experiences with the paranormal, devising what works and what doesn't from hard won trial and error.

Both the neophyte and the experienced will find a wealth of specific how-to methods to counter all forms of psychic attacks: from projections of negative thoughts from other people, to black magic curses, to hauntings by disembodied spirits, to energy sucking vampires, or attacks by demons.

Psychic Self Defense should be in the library of every psychic and serious student of the paranormal, and absolutely read by every medium, channeler, or person who makes any contact with forces, entities, or beings from the world beyond.

Psychic Self Defense is also available as an AUDIO BOOK.

22 STEPS TO THE LIGHT OF YOUR SOUL

TOP REVIEWS

This is a beautiful book. The word "generous" comes to mind. It's presented in such a way that you don't need to retain or absorb a whole lot of information at once - you can just dip into certain parts, and save others for later... so good. It opened my imagination and set my spirit spinning with possibilities and ideas. It's rare to find a book with this effect. The authors writing grabbed me from the get-go; it's charming, smooth, and intelligent without being pretentious. An amazing read. ~**Holly Wood, Amazon Top 4000 Reviewer**

There is something at work when you read the pages of this book. It feels like you are reading a dream. Not a scary dream, yet a dream where you are a little on edge. In this intimate book, the author shares with you his journey and the knowledge he has unlocked. The dream like feeling is maybe your mind awakening. I have read many of these new-age books during the past year. I can tell you that this is more advanced than many. It is challenging if you are new on your journey, yet it is fulfilling. 5/5 stars. ~**G. McFadden, Amazon Top 12,000 Reviewer**

What would it be like if you could reach through space and time to query the accumulated wisdom of the ages and get an answer to the mist vexing questions in your own life? ***22 Steps to the Light of Your Soul*** reveals such treasured insights, eloquently expounding upon the foundational principles of 22 timeless subjects of universal interest and appeal, to help each reader grow and expand into their fullest potential.

In a thought-provoking, poetic writing style, answers to questions we all ponder upon, such as love, happiness, success and friendship, are explored and illuminated in short, concise chapters, perfect for a thought to ponder through the day or contemplate as your eyes close for sleep.

Each paragraph tells a story and virtually every sentence could stand alone as an inspiring quote on your wall.

22 Steps to the Light of Your Soul is also available as an AUDIO BOOK.

LOVE YOURSELF
The Secret Key to Transforming Your Life

TOP REVIEWS

"Great book on loving yourself which is the most important part of love. Packed with wisdom and the videos are fantastic. If you want to get more out of life and be a better person to yourself, to others and the world this is a highly recommended read." **K. Allen Amazon Top 1000 Reviewer**

"Wow, is all I can say. I read this book in one sitting and I have to say that it was an amazing read. ...what the author has to say will transform your life. The 88 reasons to love were inspirational, I felt my spirit soar as I read each one." **Focusman**

Loving yourself is all about energy. As humans we devote a great deal of our energy through our time, thoughts and emotions to love. We read about it, watch movies and shows about it, dream about it, hope for it to bless our lives, feel like something critically important is lacking when it doesn't, and at the very least keep a sharp eye out for it when its missing.

Too often we look to someone else to fulfill our love and crash and burn when relationships end, or fail to live up to our fantasies of what we thought they should be. Helping those situations to never occur begins with loving yourself first. It is a precious gift from you to you. An incredibly powerful energy that not only enhances your ability to give love more fully to others, but also creates a positive energy of expanding reverberation that brings more love, friendship and appreciation to you from all directions. It is the inner light that illuminates your life empowering you to create the kind of life you desire and dream. Helping you along the way, you'll find a gift inside of 88 reasons to love yourself.

Special Bonus: Love Yourself is ALSO AVAILABLE AS AN AUDIO BOOK! This allows you to listen.

ORACLES OF CELESTINE LIGHT
Complete Trilogy Of Genesis, Nexus & Vivus

TOP REVIEWS

I I have never read a book more touching and enlightening as this Trilogy of books! This book is for anyone searching for truth in whatever form or place it may be found. It will resonate with you to your very soul if have an open mind to see it. This is what I have been searching for, the missing pieces to the puzzle, the mysteries, the deeper teachings of Yeshua. Thank you so much for sharing this treasure with the world, my life is ever enriched because of it! ~**Jamie, Amazon Top** *ts hard to describe, but reading the details of the garden of Eden, to Adam and Eve, to their banishment, was more complete and plausible than anything the bible states. For starters, it wasn't just Adam and Eve, but 12 men and 12 woman, and from them they built up the human race in the garden, and were called Edenites. This is just a small taste of the astounding history that fills in the gaps that the bible has. This book, especially for the very religious, might be hard to read, but I implore you to give it an open mind. You might just find your entire world, and spiritual view, will be opened up.* ~**Jamie, Amazon Top 1000 Reviewer**

The controversial Oracles of Celestine Light, is a portal in time to the days of Yeshua of Nazareth, over 2000 years ago, revealed in fulfilling detail to the world by the reclusive Embrosewyn Tazkuvel. It includes 155 chapters of sacred wisdom, miracles and mysteries revealing life-changing knowledge about health, longevity, happiness and spiritual expansion that reverberates into your life today.

Learn the startling, never before understood truth about: aliens, other dimensions, Atlantis, Adam & Eve, the Garden of Eden, Noah and the ark, giants, the empowerment of women, dreams, angels, Yeshua of Nazareth (Jesus), his crucifixion & resurrection, his wife Miriam of Magdala (Mary

Magdala), Yudas Iscariot (Judas), the afterlife, reincarnation, energy vortexes, witches, magic, miracles, paranormal abilities, and you!

The Oracles of Celestine Light turns accepted religious history and traditional teachings on their head. But page by page, it makes more sense than anything you've ever read and shares simple yet profound truths to make your life better today and help you to understand and unleash your miraculous potential.

The Oracles of Celestine Light explains who you are, why you are here, and your divine destiny. It is a must-read for anyone interested in spirituality, personal growth and thought-provoking answers to the unknown. Unknown

Psychic Awakening Series
CLAIRVOYANCE
BOOK 1

TOP REVIEW

For those who don't know what Clairvoyance is, check this book out and learn. Even if you don't believe it, read it anyway. I learned quite a bit more than I originally knew about it. Check it out!
~**Cayce Hrivnak, Amazon Top 15,000 Reviewer**

Would it be helpful to you if you could gain hidden knowledge about a person, place, thing, event, or concept, not by any of your five physical senses, but with visions and "knowing?" *Clairvoyance* takes you on a quest of self-discovery and empowerment, helping you unlock this potent ability in your life. It includes riveting personal stories from Embrosewyn's six decades of psychic and paranormal adventures, plus fascinating accounts of others as they discovered and cultivated their supernatural abilities.

Clearly written, step-by-step practice exercises will help you to expand and benefit from your own clairvoyant abilities. This can make a HUGE improvement in your relationships, career and creativity. As Embrosewyn has proven from over twenty years helping thousands of students to find and develop their psychic and paranormal abilities, EVERYONE, has one or more supernatural gifts. *Clairvoyance* will help you discover and unleash yours!

DREAMS
BOOK 3

TOP REVIEW

Spellbound with this book. A fantastic and informative read. ~ **Brandy**

In **Dreams**, renowned psychic/paranormal practitioner Embrosewyn Tazkuvel reveals some of his personal experiences with the transformational effect of dreams, while sharing time-tested techniques and insights that will help you unlock the power of your own night travels.

An expanded section on Lucid Dreaming gives you proven methods to induce and expand your innate ability to control your dreams. It explores the astonishing hidden world of your dream state that can reveal higher knowledge, greatly boost your creativity, improve your memory, and help you solve vexing problems of everyday life that previously seemed to have no solution.

Detailing the nine types of dreams will help you to understand which dreams are irrelevant and which you should pay close attention to, especially when they reoccur. You'll gain insight into how to interpret the various types of dreams to understand which are warnings of caution, and which are gems of inspiration that can change your life from the moment you awaken and begin to act upon that which you dreamed.

Dreaming while you sleep is a part of your daily life and cumulatively it accounts for dozens of years of your total life. It is a valuable time of far more than just rest. Become the master of your dreams and your entire life can become more than you ever imagined possible. Your dreams are the secret key to your future.

A Note From Embrosewyn About Your Soul Name

As many people who have read my books or attended my seminars over the years are aware, one of the things I use my psychic gifts for is to discover a person's Soul Name. Knowing this name and the meaning and powers of the sounds has proven to be transformational in the lives of some people. It has always been a great privilege for me to be asked to find a Soul Name for someone. But as my books have become more popular and numerous over the years, with new titles actively in the works in both the *Secret Earth series* and the *Awakening Psychic series*, plus sequels to popular stand alone books such as *Auras*, I have less and less time available to discover a Soul Name for someone when they request it. Doing so requires up to 2 hours of uninterrupted meditation time, which is a fairly great challenge for me to find these days.

With these time constraints in mind, it will generally be five to seven days once I receive your picture before I can get back to you with your Soul Name. I do hope everyone will understand. If you would like to know more about Soul Names please visit this site, *www.mysoulname.com*.

Namaste,

Embrosewyn

Before you go...one last thing

If you have enjoyed *Telekinesis*, I would be honored if you would take a few moments to revisit the book page on Amazon and leave a nice review. Thank you!

21166231R00054

Printed in Great Britain
by Amazon